Dare to Be Happy

ALSO BY HELEN LOWRIE MARSHALL

Bright Horizons

Close to the Heart

Aim for a Star

Hold to Your Dream

Dare to Be Happy

HELEN LOWRIE MARSHALL

Doubleday & Company, Inc. Garden City, New York

To
M. B. H.

With Special Thanks
to
Jane Sterling

Happy is the man who finds wisdom,
And the man who gets understanding.
—*Bible*

Library of Congress Catalog Card Number 62–13162

Printed in the United States of America
9 8 7 6 5 4

Contents

Dare to Be Happy	7
Good Morning	8
Always the Spring	9
April	9
Some Day	10
One Day at a Time	11
The Real Shame	12
Patience	13
What Can I Do	14
Heaven-Tall	15
I Shall Not Mind	15
Never the Only One	16
A Matter of Course	17
Share It	18
Thanks Giving	19
Vesper Time	19
Of What He Will	20
No Greater Sin	21
In Memory of a Friend	21
God's Will Be Done	22
Aftermath of Prayer	23
Moments of Awareness	24
And He Saw Not	25
The Wonder of It All	26
A Shaft of Sunlight	27
Next	27
Reason for Being	28
The Greatest Discovery of All	29
Almost a Memory	30
Frames of Steel	31
Follow Through	31

Masquerade 32
Living Still 33
Out Colorado Way 34
Footprints in the Snow 35
First Break 36
Weathered and Warm 37
Pop's Quartette 38
Watermelon Pickle-osophy 39
No Justice 40
Cause and Effect 41
Sam 42
The Cold Facts 43
An Ounce or Two of Heaven 44
Growing Pains 45
An Open and Shut Case 46
Ping? Pong? 47
Worth It 48
Ode to the Late Bloomer 49
Christmas List 50
Early Shopper 52
To Pamela 53
Gentle Splendor 54
Christmas Eve 55
The Most Beautiful Christmas 56
Christmas Alone 58
Christmas Miracle 59
High Time 60
The Week Before Christmas 62
The Song and the Echo 64

Dare to Be Happy

Dare to be happy—don't shy away,
Reach out and capture the joy of Today!

Life is for living! Give it a try;
Open your heart to that sun in the sky.

Dare to be loving, and trusting, and true;
Treasure the hours with those dear to you.

Dare to be kind—it's more fun than you know;
Give joy to others, and watch your own grow.

Dare to admit all your blessings, and then
Every day count them all over again.

Dare to be happy, don't be afraid—
This is the day which the Lord hath made!

Good Morning

"Good Morning!" What a lovely way
To open up a brand new day!
Not knowing what that day may hold–
A sun of tinsel or of gold–
The phrase embraces in its scope
The whole of man's eternal hope;
His faith–of every soul a part;
The love that lives in every heart.
"Good Morning–and a Good Today!
May all things happy come your way;
And may the light of this new dawn
Find all your cares and worries gone."
So much the simple words convey–
"Good Morning–It's a lovely day!"

Always the Spring

Life has its seasons—its bright summer days,
Its autumns made poignant with memories' haze,
Its cold, lonely winters when bitter winds blow—
But always the crocus of Hope in the snow.

Always the day when the morning breaks through
And clouds break away to a skyful of blue.
Life has its seasons—its sun and its rain,
Its winter—but always the springtime again!

April

There's a feeling of promise in the air,
A feeling of promise everywhere—
A promise of singing birds and bees,
A promise of fruit on barren trees;

A promise of gardens blooming gay,
A promise of summer come one day,
A promise of warm and sunny skies,
A promise that nothing ever dies.

A promise of beauty yet unseen,
A promise of brown earth clothed in green,
A promise of warmth and light and cheer
A promise of hope this time of year.

Some Day

At least half the fun
Is in wanting a thing—
The longing, the dreaming.
Although life may bring
An endless procession
Of chore after chore,
There's no one to say
That the heart may not soar!

There's a pure touch of magic
That brightens the way
And lightens the load
In the two words, "Some day."
"Some day!" the heart whispers,
And flings its hope high—
As bright, as remote
As a star in the sky.

But a star that's your own,
Though it be eons far,
Is special, and different
From just any star.
And some day—who knows?
(There's that magic again!)
And you've all the fun
Of the dreaming till then.

One Day at a Time

I'm glad life is given us bit by bit,
  In minutes, and days, and years;
For if we were faced with the whole of it
  How filled it would be with fears;
With all of its laughter, and all of its pain,
  Its sorrow and joy and care—
Why, even its beauty all at one time
  Would be more than we could bear.

But God drops a bit of happiness here,
  And lowers a shadow there,
And each of us has his portion of both,
  The bitter and the fair.
And, whether the way be rough or fine,
  It's a comforting thing to know
We've only one step to take at a time,
  Just one little day to go.

The Real Shame

You say you have acted foolishly,
Your days are filled with remorse;
That the shame of this one foolish act
Has altered your whole life's course.

But may I say that the real shame lies
In steeping yourself in regret.
The lesson should be remembered—yes,
But, as for the rest—forget.

Shame is a scavenger—it preys
On deeds that are dead and gone.
The only real fool is the fool who won't try
To pick himself up and go on.

Patience

"Things have a way of working out,"
My father used to say.
"Don't force the issue. Do your best
And work and wait and pray."

How many times those words return
When life's a tangled thread–
"Just do your best today, and leave
To God the days ahead."

Somewhere a Master Planner works,
Though how we may not know,
But in due time things will work out–
The years have proved it so.

What Can I Do

What can I do—only one—
When such great tasks need to be done?
Right wrestles wrong upon the brink—
What can I do?
                    I can think.

What can I do—only I?
War clouds hang heavy in the sky;
So grave the problems of today—
What can I do?
                    I can pray.

What can I do—just one vote?
Can strength lie in so weak a note?
Yet—one voice shouting from the peak
Will carry far—
                    And I can speak.

Heaven-Tall

I'm such a little person, Lord,
  So very small,
Yet when I reach my soul to Thee,
  I'm Heaven-tall.

My tasks are all so trivial,
  Such drudgery,
Yet each is touched with nobleness
  When done for Thee.

A lifetime seems so empty-short,
  The hours flee—
Yet in Thy hands life reaches to
  Eternity.

I Shall Not Mind

If I can face toward the sunset so—
Head high and steady step, though it be slow,
An understanding heart, an open mind,
Abiding faith in good of all mankind;
A sense of kindly humor, fresh and keen,
A reverence deep toward the Great Unseen;
If I can go thus toward the skies of gold,
I shall not mind this thing of growing old.

Never the Only One

You say you've the right
To live your own life.
The right—yes—the privilege, too;
But never forget that
That life you call yours
Is a life that was given to you.

It's a life that was nurtured
And sheltered and loved
When you were too small to know,
And your need for that love
And that someone to care
You never will quite outgrow.

So live your own life—
It's your privilege, your right,
But always remember, my son,
That life is an inter-
Twining of lives—
You're never the only one;

And the good and the true
And the fine things you do,
As well as the mean and the small,
Will all leave their mark
On the lives around you—
Your life is a part of them all.

A Matter of Course

He followed the right, as a matter of course,
And I would venture to say
That he never once stopped to reason why
The right was the better way.

He helped where he could, as a matter of course,
And I doubt if he once gave a thought
To the credit he'd get for the good that he did—
Wrong was simply a thing to be fought.

God grant that our sons, as a matter of course,
Will champion all that is good;
That the course we have tried to set for them
Will lead them to do as they should.

That their sense of duty will be submerged
By that stronger and warmer force
Of love, that makes duty a natural thing,
And right just a matter of course.

Share It

If grief is yours,
Turn to a friend and share it;
An understanding heart
Will help you bear it.
And if joy fills your heart
Let others share
Your happiness, as well
As your despair.

If faith is yours,
A peace profound and deep,
Let it not be a secret
That you keep
Enshrined, but shrouded,
In your inmost heart—
Tell others, let the whole world
Have a part.

Thanks Giving

I tried—I tried so very hard to pray,
To thank God for this lovely, lovely day;
But, as I knelt, so many blessings grew,
It seemed as though my heart would burst in two
With thankfulness—so many blessings there
To crowd into just one small "Thank you" prayer;
But as my lips groped haltingly to find
The words to speak my humbly grateful mind,
I heard God's gentle whisper, kneeling there,
"Arise my child, thy heart said thy prayer."

Vesper Time

Soft, low,
The organ plays,
And muted sun bestows
A benedictive touch to each
Bowed head.

Of What He Will

How haloed are the joys of Yesterday
Through misty mauve of memory defined;
How gently time erases, dims the way
That things unpleasant may be lost to mind;
How zealously the heart guards fleeting pleasure
And casts aside the bitterness and pain;
Looks back to Yesterday to find its measure
For building up its hope and faith again.
How tenderly the Father has provided
The soul of man with liberty to choose—
To find the good in all the many-sided,
And salvage that of life he can best use.
  The Past stands by, a bank where man may borrow
  Of what he will to shape his own Tomorrow.

No Greater Sin

There is no greater sin than this,
That one, with talent blest,
Should settle for the good-enough,
Who might have done the best.

In Memory of a Friend

Each day she would awaken
With a bright "Good Morning, Lord",
And thank Him for another lovely day;
And then, serenely cheerful, she
Would turn her thoughts toward
The homely little tasks that fell her way.

How glorious the morning
And how thrilled she must have been
When she awoke to find herself Up There
And, face to face, to wish
That Friend of hers, "Good Morning, Lord",
And thank Him with her usual morning prayer.

God's Will Be Done

"It is God's will," he meekly said
And bowed a weak, submissive head.
Folding his hands with passive grace,
He yielded his place in life's race.
"There is no more that I can do;
My life has ended—I am through."
His face turned toward the setting sun,
Vanquished, he said—"God's will be done."

His brother said, "It is God's will
That I continue useful still.
Perhaps I cannot work or live
The same, but I have much to give.
God has not willed this pain of mine;
These handicaps are not divine.
They are man-made. God wills the good.
Life is not always understood,
But I believe God wills that I
Should keep on serving till I die."
His face turned toward the *rising* sun
With eager zeal—"God's will be done!"

Aftermath of Prayer

When I pray for my neighbor across the sea,
And he, in turn, intercedes for me;
When all of God's children everywhere
Join in the common bond of prayer;
When hearts are turned to thoughts of others,
Then will the nations meet as brothers.

For war is based on a selfish creed
That has no care for a neighbor's need,
But peace is born of a will to share—
The clear, sure aftermath of prayer.

Moments of Awareness

So much of life we all pass by
With heedless ear, and careless eye.
Bent with our cares we plod along,
Blind to the beauty, deaf to the song.

But moments there are when we pause to rest
And turn our eyes from the goal's far crest.
We become aware of the wayside flowers,
And sense God's hand in this world of ours.

We hear a refrain, see a rainbow's end,
Or we look into the heart of a friend.
We feel at one with mankind. We share
His griefs and glories, joy and care.

The sun flecks gold thru the sheltering trees,
And we shoulder our burdens with twice the ease.
Peace and content and a world that sings
The moment of true awareness brings.

And He Saw Not

He boasted unbelief,
And scorned the Deity–
  And all the while he sat beneath
  A flowering apple tree.

He said there was no proof
Of God–that no one knows–
  And all the while he idly smelled
  The fragrance of a rose.

He scoffed at pious folk
Who prattle of God's grace–
  And all the while he looked into
  A baby's upturned face.

The Wonder of It All

There are so many small, incessant things—
The constant whir of tiny unseen wings,
The steady beat of hearts too small to hear—
That never reach the conscious eye or ear.

The crack of seedlings breaking through the pod.
The tender grasses pushing through the sod;
The bustle of the world down underground,
The air above so full of soundless sound.

A world within a world, where lives repeat
Their own small cycles, infinite, complete,
The unseen, steady flow of death and birth—
The business of an ever changing earth.

The order and the wonder of it all—
A universe so great—a world so small!

A Shaft of Sunlight

A shaft of sunlight breaking through
Can make the whole world shining new;
Can shape tomorrow, change a life;
Can banish doubt and fear and strife.

One shaft of sunlight through the grey—
One word of cheer that we may say,
Could carry farflung consequence,
And might make all the difference.

Next

Your turn may be next,
Always keep that in mind.
Be patient, and one of these days
You will find
Your ship in the harbor there
Waiting for you,
And, suddenly, all of your dreams
Will come true.
So, never by others'
Good fortune be vexed.
Be happy they're happy—
Your turn may be next.

Reason for Being

I would look deep within
This living book I call Myself.
I would dust off the cover,
Lift it down from Life's high shelf;
Would delve deep into chapters
That long ago were closed,
And bring to light the secrets
Never honestly exposed.
I would study it for lessons
That should be recorded there.
I would test it for its value—
Is it honest? Is it fair?
I would search to find the answer
Why this book is on Life's shelf—
I would hope to find the reason
For this book I call Myself.

The Greatest Discovery of All

Nation vies with nation,
And man surpasses man
Discovering new stairways
  To the stars.
Science builds on science,
Trained mind commands skilled hand
In earthman's race toward
  The moon and Mars.

Discovery! Discovery!
To find the best—or worst!
And brother tramples brother
  At its call;
No sacrifice too great if he
Can only be the first
To find the greatest wonder
  Of them all.

But woman smiles with woman
Across the whole wide earth,
For every mother-heart there
  Understands,
The greatest of discoveries,
Of farthest-reaching worth
Is when her baby finds
  His own two hands.

Almost a Memory

What is it that the song awakes in me?
Almost a tear—almost a memory;
A fleeting, lonely something that evades,
A glimmering of memory that fades
And vanishes as I pursue—and yet,
Something it is my heart cannot forget.

What is this haunting thing within the strain
That stirs some deep, long buried, hidden pain
Within the heart of me—a yearning there?
My groping fingers clutch the empty air,
The ghost uncaptured, unrevealed—and yet,
Something it is my heart cannot forget.

And now the song has ended—quiet falls,
And I am left still wandering the halls
Of reverie, lost in my fruitless quest
Of half-remembered things locked in my breast.
What is it that the song awakes in me?
Almost a tear—almost a memory.

Frames of Steel

Some dreams, be they night or day,
Brightly appear, but briefly stay—
Flit through the mind on butterfly wings,
Fragile, elusive, impractical things.

Others are made of sterner stuff—
Wings with a texture strong and tough.
These are the dreams that linger on
Night after night and dawn upon dawn.
These are the dreams that dare to see
Man and his world as they ought to be.
Dreams with wings that turn the wheel
Of Progress—wings with frames of steel!

Follow Through

Put your best foot forward,
You've talent—then show it.
How else is the world
Ever going to know it?
But—one word of caution—
Success depends, too,
On how well your every-day foot
Follows through.

Masquerade

Mother Nature's preparing for one last fling,
  A wonderful masquerade ball!
Each tree is determined to win the prize
  For the handsomest costume of all.

The aspen's a princess in golden lace,
  A beautiful, shimmering sight;
The maple, resplendent in crimson cape,
  Her gallant and dashing knight.

The sumac in feathery Indian plumes
  Of yellow and red and brown,
Are crouched on the hills like tawny braves
  Surrounding the sleepy town.

Mother Nature is planning a masquerade,
  One final and glorious fling,
Then she'll settle down under her blanket of snow
  And doze, content, until Spring.

Living Still

A garden is a growing thing.
  Each day, each passing hour,
Some bit of newness there unfolds—
  A leaf, a bud, a flower.
A garden is a living thing,
  And even when the snow
Has blanketed its silent form
  It does not cease to grow,
For every tender seedling there,
  Each hard, encrusted pod,
Contains a tiny spark of life,
  A living bit of God.

Life, also, is a growing thing;
  Each day, each passing hour,
Finds something new unfolding there—
  New thoughts, new strength, new power.
And when the snows of sorrow come,
  As snows of sorrow will,
The seeds of Hope lie dormant then
  But go on living still.
And, just as Spring returns to bring
  The garden fresh new leaves—
So does the Spring of Life return
  To every heart that grieves.

Out Colorado Way

Have you come to see the mountains,
Come to see and know the mountains?
Have you come to love the mountains
  Out Colorado way?

Have you wandered through the aspens,
On a trail up through the aspens,
Heard the shy and whispering aspens
  Imploring you to stay?

Have you watched beside the waters,
The rushing, tumbling waters,
The quiet, crystal waters
  Where dappled rainbows play?

Have you known the spell of pine trees,
The spicy smell of pine trees,
The lullaby of pine trees
  As they softly sway?

Have you listened to the stillness,
The solemn, peaceful stillness,
The deep, cathedral stillness
  That makes you want to pray?

Have you felt the awesome grandeur,
The overwhelming grandeur,
From the heights, the splendid grandeur
  Stretching far out and away?

Have you come to see the mountains,
The misty, purple mountains,
The majestic, snow-capped mountains
  Out Colorado way?

Footprints in the Snow

Spring tiptoed thru the town last night,
Disguised in robes of winter-white.
This morning she seems far away—
The wind so cold—the skies so grey—
But there are signs that prove it so,
Small crocus footprints in the snow!

First Break

Come along, Toby-dog, you poor, lonesome pup,
You can't understand—little boys must grow up.

I know it must seem very heartless and cruel
To keep you at home on his first day at school.

I'll tell you a secret, though, Toby, my lad,
My own heart is not feeling overly glad.

He left me home, too. So big he has grown,
So big—but so little to start off alone.

No use, though, to whimper and lie there in wait,
That same little boy won't come back thru that gate.

He'll be inches taller, and broader of view,
And never again quite the baby we knew.

So come along, Toby, there's work to be done.
He belongs to the world now—your master—my son.

Weathered and Warm

Give me an older house for my late years,
With mellowed charm that only time can bring;
Weathered and warm with memories that cling,
And where faint aura of past love adheres.
New houses are for brides. Some bride's young fears,
Her hopes through trying winters, joy of spring,
Have helped to give this house of mine that thing
Intangible, yet real, that so endears.
Now, were I younger, I would doubtless view
With some distaste, its quaint, old air of rest,
But youth for both of us is long since spent,
And when the morning sun comes pouring through
Its ancient window panes—deep in my breast
I share with my old house its sweet content.

Pop's Quartette

When I was just a shaver—
Seems no more than yesterday—
The one thing always guaranteed
To make me stop my play
And just sit still and listen
Till it ended all too soon,
Was when Pop's quartette practiced
On a Sunday afternoon.

They always met at our house,
'Cause Ma could follow along
And chord on the piano
With most any kind of song.
Pop sang the baritone
And beat the time—I see him yet.
How proud I was to have a Pop
Who led his own quartette!

And how I loved their harmonizing
Of "Sweet Adeline,"
The soulful way they warbled
In "Sweetheart, Say You'll Be Mine."
But when they sang the sea songs—
"Yo-ho-ho, to sea we go!"
Pretending they were sailors,
Well, for me that topped the show!

Now all are gone—my mother, too,
The sailors put to sea,
But oh, how often I recall
The joy they gave to me,
And hope, somewhere, they're harmonizing
Some celestial tune,
The way they always used to
On a Sunday afternoon.

Watermelon Pickle-osophy

A watermelon sort of makes you
Think of Life, itself—
Sometimes the years 'left over'
After we're put 'on the shelf'
Turn out to be the sweetest—
Even sweeter than those years
When we were deep in youth's
Pink, sugary dreams up to our ears!
Those rosy hours that we devoured
With youth's impetuous haste—
The very heart of Life consumed
With scarcely time to taste!
Now, that my autumn years are here,
It's mighty nice, I find,
To just sit back and savor
All the goodness of the rind!

No Justice

Now, me, I've got insurance—
Fire, accident and theft,
A life insurance policy
To comfort the bereft.

I've burial protection,
And insurance on the flivver,
And disability, in case
I should have Grandpaw's liver.

I've got my crops protected
Against cyclones and hail;
I've got myself protection
If my crops should ever fail.

I haven't missed a doggone thing,
I've gone insurance poor—
But do I ever cash in on
This stuff I'm paying for?

Not once have I been burglarized;
My house has never burned;
A cyclone came right at me once,
But 'fore it hit, it turned.

The year the crops were all hailed out
The blamed hail skirted mine.
And next year when the crops all failed,
My own came through just fine.

I've never been sick in my life,
My liver's never tender;
I've never had an accident
Or even bent a fender.

For all the years I've paid and paid
So I could be protected,
It sure don't seem fair, somehow,
That I've never once collected!

Cause and Effect

Once, someone said something nice about me,
And, all undeserved though I knew it to be,
I treasured it there on my heart's deepest shelf,
Till one day I quite surprised even myself
By honestly making an effort to be
That nice thing that somebody said about me!

Sam

Sam was always very busy
With a million things to do;
Running this way, running that way,
Never finished, never through;
With a million little problems,
And a million trifling cares;
Always hurried, always worried,
With his day-to-day affairs;
Never happy with his labors,
Never time to do his best—
Always busy, busy, busy,
Never time for any rest.

On his tombstone it was written
When, at last, Sam had to go—
"So busy buying peanuts
He completely missed the show."

The Cold Facts

The first snow of the season
  Is a lovely sight to see,
And the bard in me responds to it
  In sheerest ecstasy.

But when that same snow lies around
  For weeks, collecting grime,
My Muses cease their musing,
  And my thoughts don't run to rhyme.

That quaint, romantic music
  Of the tires' icy squeak
Fails to rouse my fervor, somehow,
  When my joints begin to creak.

And I've come to this conclusion—
  That poems praising snow
Are not composed in winter
  When it's twenty-some below.

I'll wager ninety-nine per cent
  Of wintry gems are made
In a hammock, in mid-summer,
  When it's ninety in the shade.

An Ounce or Two of Heaven

I should like to buy a perfume,
Nothing fancy, something plain—
I had in mind the scent
Of city streets washed clean with rain;
Or, possibly, the fragrance
Of a baby freshly tubbed;
Or the spicy, heady odor
Of green mint leaves crushed and rubbed;
Do you have that grand aroma
Found in fresh-baked home-made bread?
Or the luxury-laden fragrance
Of clean sheets upon a bed?
How about the smell of bacon,
Crisp and brown and sizzling good?
Or the dreamy, smokey odor
Of a fire in the wood?
Perhaps you have the crispy
Smell of autumn in the air,
Or that more seductive fragrance
Of a spring day, soft and rare—
I should like to buy a perfume,
Any simple scent will do—
Just an ounce or two of Heaven
Made up in an earthly brew.

Growing Pains

I'm muddled and befuddled,
Just can't figure it all out–
Facts I thought invincible,
I now look on with doubt.

The deeper my mind penetrates,
The more the questions rise.
Those nice, complacent platitudes,
My present self denies.

They tell me doubts are growing pains
And no cause for alarm–
That healthy curiosity
Can do the truth no harm.

I should be glad, I guess,
That I am growing less naive,
But it would help if I could know
Just what I do believe.

An Open and Shut Case

Some bad fairies must have listened
When my young son was christened,
And placed upon his head
  A special curse.
Though mostly he's quite normal,
Easy-going and informal,
In this one thing he reasons
  In reverse!

When the day is hot as blazes
My pleading never fazes;
Invariably, he shuts the door
  With care.
I simply can't get through to him—
The whole idea seems new to him
That in the summer we could use
  Some air!

But—really it's uncanny—
Now, when every nook and cranny
Is a lurking place for winter's
  Drafts and cold,
In he breezes with the weather,
Door left open altogether—
No matter how I threaten,
  Scream and scold.

He must have some queer reason
To so reverse the season.
Psychologists might ferret
  Out the core;
But me—I'm just his parent;
All I hope, it's not inherent—
Excuse me, please—Hey, Junior,
  Shut the door!

Ping? Pong?

A hint to harried housewives,
  A helpful one, I hope—
A watermelon should be thumped;
  You sniff a cantaloupe.

I wouldn't think of buying one
  Without this little ritual.
With me, it's a procedure that
  Has come to be habitual.

Of course, I cannot guarantee
  Your choice will be correct,
But it will make those less informed
  Eye you with great respect.

As for myself, I must admit
  It doesn't mean a thing.
I've no idea how it should smell
  Or how it ought to ping!

Worth It

Saint Peter, when my salesgirl
Stands before the Pearly Gates,
Don't keep her out because the Book
Says she prevaricates.
She only honeys up her words
Because she's learned it pays
With folks like me, who simply purr
And purchase at her praise!

When I try on a size thirteen
And nearly burst the seams,
I lose ten pounds and fifteen years
As she stands there and beams.
"My deah, that dress was *made* for you!
Your figure's so petite,
So chic, so smart–divine, my deah!
It's really too, too sweet!"

And so I buy the thing,
But what I pay for is morale.
She sends me on my way convinced
That I'm some nifty gal.
So–please don't be too hard on her,
Although you know, I guess,
That dress she said was so divine–
It really is a mess.

Ode to the Late Bloomer

Hail to thee, Black Bloomer,
  Dark memory of the past;
How well thy sheath of chaste sateen
  Did fend the wintry blast!

How sturdily, how sensibly
  Thy style and substance stood,
A symbol of that by-gone day
  Of sheltered womanhood.

So snugly close below the knee,
  So ample in the rear—
How thou must shudder at today's
  Brief undies, scant and sheer!

Now to the ragbag, ignominious
  Fate hast thou consigned—
The spurned, cast-off protector
  Of ungrateful womankind!

Christmas List

Along about December first
Ma gets her tablet out,
And it ain't hard to figure
What it is that she's about.

She'll set there with her eyes
A-starin' far off into space,
With memories a-chasin'
Little smiles around her face;

And then she'll scribble down a name,
Or, maybe, three or four,
Then set and dream a while again
And scribble down some more.

I tried suggestin' once
We save the list from year to year;
But it was plain that Ma
Just didn't hold with that idear.

"Why, Pa," she said, "if we did that
We'd miss the nicest part.
A Christmas card's no good at all
Lest it comes from the heart.

"When I make out a list each year
I think of every one,
And I remember all the nice things
Each one's said and done.

"You mark my word, cards sent this way
Will mean a heap sight more
Than if we hustled through a list
We'd made some year before."

I reckon that she's right,
'Cause then I get to thinkin', too,
And it's surprisin' how the memories
Come a-crowdin' through—

A heap o' happy memories
That we'd a-likely missed
If Ma had not insisted
On a brand new Christmas list.

Early Shopper

This year, I told myself, I would sit back,
Hands folded, brow serene and tension slack,
And watch the frenzied Christmas horde rush by—
They who hadn't been as wise as I!

And so, on summer days when others lay
In hammocks, I pursued my stealthy way
In leisure through each cool, uncrowded store,
And purchased Christmas presents by the score.

Long months before the Christmas rush began,
My gifts were wrapped and ready, spick and span.
I could enjoy the sparkle and the glitter
For once, without my nerve ends all a-twitter.

And now I roam the aisles—onlooker only—
And view the gift displays, a trifle lonely.
Although I know I'm winner in the game—
Still, somehow, Christmas isn't quite the same.

And I still have one problem to contend with,
One I'd no idea my smart plan would end with—
The awful thought keeps running through my head,
"Oh dear, I wish now I'd got that, instead!"

To Pamela

Such misery you seldom see
In little girls not quite twice three.
The big round tears were there because—
  "There isn't any Santa Claus—
  No fairies, elves, or anything!"
The words have such a hopeless ring.

Poor tyke, her world so rainbow bright
Has turned to grown-up black and white.
I wish that I could make her see
That fairies never cease to be;
And Santa Claus will never leave
The heart that chooses to believe
In miracles of love; that elves
Are always present in ourselves—
Some good, some not so good, that's true,
That make us do the things we do.

So, Darling, keep your Santa Claus;
Don't ever let him go, because
This old world needs so very much
The magic of Old Santa's touch.
Hold fast your dreams and don't you grieve—
They're real as long as you believe;
And never underrate their worth
In spreading peace—goodwill on earth.

Gentle Splendor

There's a sort of gentle splendor
Shining out on every hand
For him who has the eye to see,
The heart to understand.

I have seen it in the patience
Of a mother with her brood;
And in the helping hand stretched out
To one not understood.

I have seen it in the eyes of one
Bone-weary with the strain,
Who puts his shoulder to the wheel
And tries and tries again.

I have seen it in the act of spreading
Love's protective cloak
Across the ugly words laid down
By thoughtless, unkind folk.

It's the sort of gentle splendor
That I like to think shone out
On that night within the stable
With the angels all about.

The sort of gentle splendor that
  Enwrapped the Christ Child there—
Still encircling truth and beauty,
  Love and courage everywhere.

Christmas Eve

There's a glitter, and a litter
And bells ringing everywhere;
And the strains of sacred music
Floating through the frosty air.
There's a light in every window
And a light in every eye,
And out there toward the eastward
There's a Star up in the sky.

There's a glory and a sadness
All mixed up inside the heart,
And a loving there so fierce
That it tears the soul apart.
A magic night of miracles
Of peace, goodwill and joy—
A busy world remembering
The birthday of a Boy.

The Most Beautiful Christmas

I think the most beautiful Christmas
  That I shall ever know
Was a Christmas Eve in a little church
  A long, long time ago.

I was one of the cherubs,
  Dressed in a long, white gown,
With a beautiful pair of cheesecloth wings
  And a halo that kept slipping down.

And I knelt with the other cherubs
  By a crude box filled with hay,
But to me it was really the manger
  Where the dearest of Babies lay.

And Mary was there, and Joseph—
  Mary so gentle and sweet,
And small Kings dressed in bathrobes
  Laid gifts at the Baby's feet.

The shepherds knelt to worship Him,
  The newborn King divine,
And the church was soft with candlelight,
  Sweet with the smell of pine.

Up in one corner of the loft
  A single star shone bright,
And somewhere in the dimness
  Voices sang "O Holy Night".

It was one of those rare moments
  That seem to strike a chime,
And the memory of its beauty
  Lingers on each Christmas time.

Now, children's children trail the robes,
  And wear the cheesecloth wings,
And I smile at the memories
  The dear old story brings,

And wonder if their tender hearts,
  So eager to believe,
Are sensing all the beauty
  As I did that Christmas Eve.

Christmas Alone

Tonight I trim the tree—with memories—
Small, heart-framed miniatures of other trees,
And other Christmas Eves, and other years.
I even hang a few bright, glistening tears,
For even happy memories are a part
Of loneliness. The corners of the heart
Are packed with memories of every kind,
But Christmas always brings the best to mind.

I rest before the fire burning low,
And see small ghostly stockings in a row.
I kiss each long-gone little sleepy-head
And watch them troop, reluctant, off to bed.
Now carolers come singing in the night.
I listen—"All is calm"—yes, all is bright.
I breathe a prayer of thanks for memory
And place the shining star atop my tree.

Christmas Miracle

With heavy heart I listened
As carolers sang out,
Rebelling at the words
Of peace and joy they sang about.

For me there was no peace, no joy,
No sense of Christmas cheer;
My saddened heart so filled with pain
And loneliness and fear.

And then, through tear-filled eyes I saw
The Christmas Star on high,
A star my tears had softened
To a cross there in the sky.

A cross—the symbol of God's love,
Shone through my grief and loss.
Had I not known the tears,
I might have never seen the cross.

Miraculously then, I felt
A sense of sweet release,
And, gratefully, my heart received
The wonder of His peace.

High Time

Now, Santa is a fine old man,
Believe me, I'm all for him;
So generous, so jolly—
It's no wonder kids adore him.
I'd be the last to sell him short,
I've loved him all my life;
But I do think it's time we gave
Some credit to his wife!

Who makes those Christmas goodies?
It's no bewhiskered elf!
And did you ever see a Christmas
Tree that trimmed itself?
Who bakes those luscious fruitcakes
And cookies by the dozen—
Remembers every friend and every
Uncle, aunt and cousin?

Who writes the cards and thank-you notes?
Not one does she forget.
If Santa had to send them
They'd, no doubt, be waiting yet!
Who shops and shops for Santa
Till she can hardly stand?
And who transforms the house into
A Christmas fairyland?

Who wraps the gifts that Santa brings,
So beautiful to see?
Who knows exactly what to get
For each, instinctively?
Who makes wings for the angels
And drills the Christmas play,
Presides at Christmas parties,
Always gracious, always gay?

Who makes each childhood Christmas
A hallowed memory?
Who still makes Christmas Christmas
For the likes of you and me?
Old Saint Nick? Well, he helps, that's true,
We love him at our house;
But there's another Christmas saint—
Old Santa's faithful spouse!

The Week Before Christmas

'Tis the week before Christmas
And all through the house
Are socks full of holes
As if chewed by a mouse,
And shirts minus buttons
And rips that need sewing.
The things that need doing
Keep growing and growing!
My basket of mending
Is stacked by my chair
In hopes that I might
Find a minute to spare.
My husband's a martyr
With holes in his heels;
My children existing
On unbalanced meals.
We grab a quick snack
When and where we are able—
I'm doing the cards
On the dining room table.
The neighbors are thinking,
I strongly suspect,
That mine is a family
Of want and neglect;
While I with my conscience
Am wrestling each night

Because I've a sneaking
Suspicion they're right!
But then, all at once,
The last card has been sent,
The gifts are all wrapped,
And the money all spent!
The fruitcake is aging,
The tree gay and bright,
The choir at church
Singing "O Holy Night".
The lights in the windows,
The love and the cheer—
You know it's the most
Precious time of the year.
We sit by the fire
And gaze at the coals.
Who cares if the stockings there
Have a few holes!
It's Christmas Eve now,
Everything is all right—
Merry Christmas to all,
And to all a Good Night!

The Song and the Echo

A song we sing. We cannot know
How far the sound of it will go,
How long its echo will be heard.
We can but pray that every word,
Each note in this, the song we sing,
Will find its resting place and bring
Some little measure of repose,
Some strength, some happiness to those
Who hear our song. If just one smiles
To hear its echo down the miles,
Then we should be content and know
Our song was meant—God willed it so.